YEOWWW

YAP ARF YAP

Second Printing — January, 1977
Third Printing — January, 1981
Original Illustrations for *TA for Tots* by JoAnn Dick

Published by Jalmar Press, Inc.
6501 Elvas Avenue
Sacramento, California 95819
ISBN: 0-915190-33-8

Hi! I'm Dr. Freed.

This book is more than just a coloring book. For one thing, you'll meet all the delightful characters you've loved in TA for TOTS. You'll meet Warm Fuzzies, Cold Pricklies and Prinzes who live in the Land of OK.

And, just like in TA for TOTS, every one of the human people and animal people you color will help you feel good. That's what's important — for you to feel good — for you to feel OK. You are an important person. There's no one else quite like you. You have a perfect right to feel happy, sad or even to be angry.

Maurice the Turtle is waiting at the bottom of this page. He wants to take you on a fun tour to meet our friends and Prinzes. Color them any color you wish. Have a Warm Fuzzy time.

Be sure and write and tell me about your coloring fun tour.

Dr. Freed

Right this way, Prinzes

Come to OK Land and paint all my friends happy with your trusty crayons or watercolors.

You can give Fuzzies and get Fuzzies.

Hippo and I give lots of Warm Fuzzies to each other.

Cold Pricklies make you feel Frozzy. Not OK.

She feels O.K.! Lots of Warm Fuzzies.
A Prinz in OK Land.

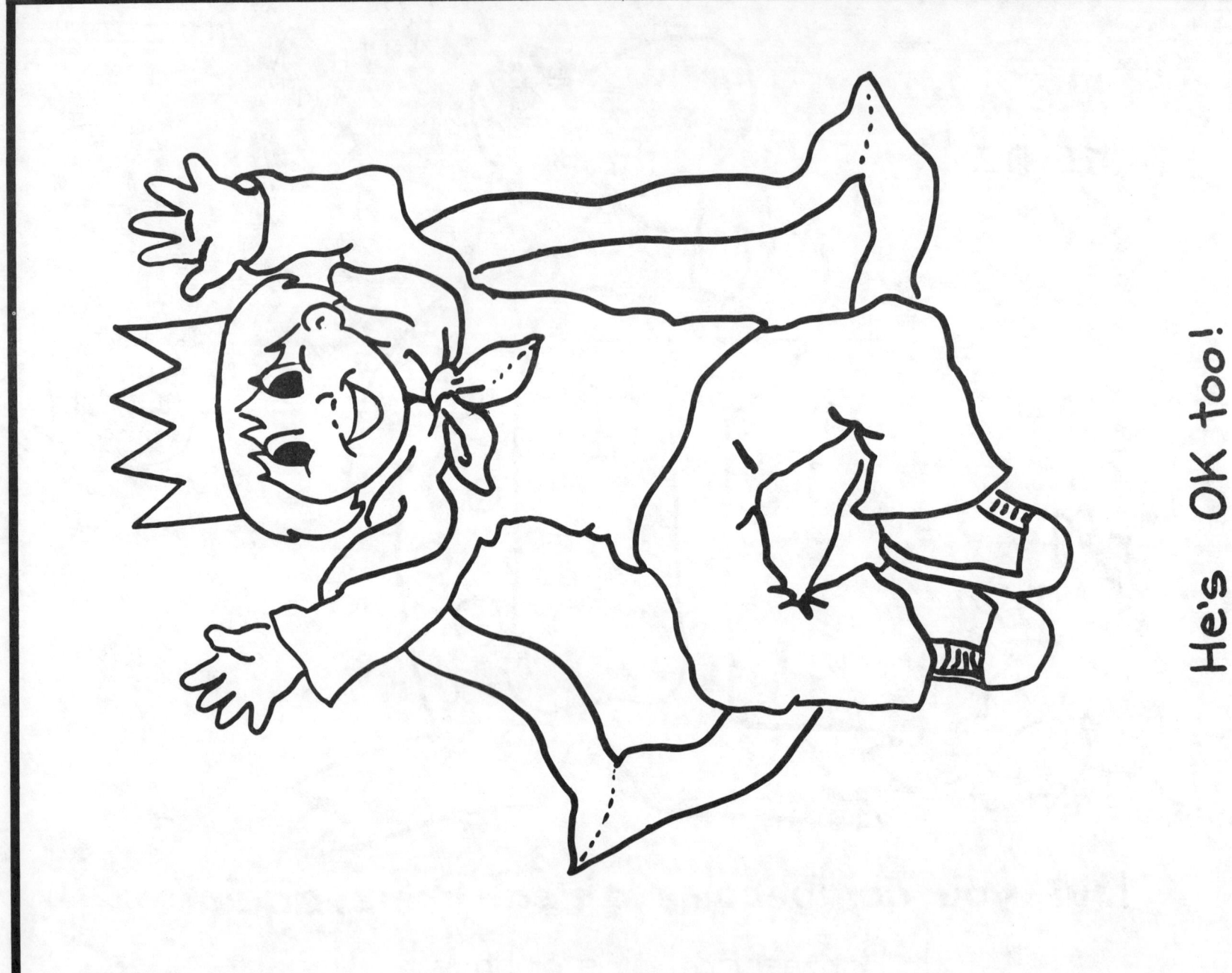

He's OK too!
Another Prinz in OK Land.

Everybody can be a Prinz.

It's good to just be You.

Warm Fuzzy times are the best times.

My friend Irving gives and gets lots of Warm Fuzzies.

Sometimes we all feel
Frozzy.

It's more fun to feel
Prinzy!

I feel Prinzy!

Keep Cold Pricklies Out.

JALMAR PRESS, INC.   INDIVIDUAL ORDER FORM

6501 Elvas Avenue
Sacramento, CA 95819
(916) 451-2897

MINIMUM ORDER: $10.00
Shipping and Handling Charges:
Under $15.00 .... $1.75
$15.00 to $20.00 .... $2.25
Over $20.00 .... $2.75
TOT PAC or KID PAC $4.00

Bill To _____

Street _____
City _____ State ____ Zip ____
PO # _____ Date _____
☐ Master Charge ☐ BankAmericard/Visa
Account # _____
Expiration Date _____
Signature _____

Ship To _____

Street _____
City _____ State ____ Zip ____

Order	NEW 1981 RELEASES from JALMAR	Retail
	Tots in OKayland, USA 1982 Calendar	$5.95
	Pitching In PB 0-915190-31-1	$4.95
	RECENT 1980 RELEASES	
	Cooking on a Woodburning Stove PB 0-915190-28-1	$7.95
	First Time Out PB 0-915190-26-5	$5.95
	Natural Breast Enlargement PB 0-915190-30-3	$6.95
	With Cassette	$16.90
	Please Keep on Smoking! We Need the Money PB 0-915190-27-3	$2.95
	TA for Tots, Vol II* PB 0-915190-25-7	$8.95
	When Apples Ain't Enough PB 0-915190-24-9	$4.95
	BACKLIST	
	Finding Hidden Treasure PB 0-915190-16-8	$6.95
	Hope for the Frogs PB 0-915190-17-6	$3.95
	Joy of Backpacking PB 0-915190-06-0	$5.95
	The Original Warm Fuzzy Tale PB 0-915190-08-7	$3.95
	Pajamas Don't Matter PB 0-915190-21-4	$5.95
	The Parent Book PB 0-915190-15-X	$9.95

Order	BACKLIST (cont.)	Retail
	Reach for the Sky PB 0-915190-13-3	$7.95
	TA for Kids (3rd Edition)* PB 0-915190-09-5	$4.95
	TA for Management PB 0-915190-05-2	$6.95
	TA for Teens* PB 0-915190-03-6	$7.95
	TA for Tots (And Other Prinzes)* PB 0-915190-12-5	$5.95
	Spanish Ed 0-915190-12-5	$8.95
	Reduced Rate: TA for TOTS plus TA for TOTS Volume II for only: $16.00	$16.00
	TA for Tots Coloring Book PB 0-915190-33-8	$1.95
	SPIRIT MASTERS for TA for Tots Coloring Book PB 0-915190-18-4	$3.95
	A Time to Teach, A Time to Dance HC 0-915190-04-4	$4.95
	The Warm Fuzzy Song Book PB 0-915190-14-1	$8.95
	A-V MULTIMEDIA PACS	$3.95
	KIDPAC	$165.00
	TOT PAC ☐ Filmstrips ☐ Slides	$135.00
	FUN PAC	$14.95
	PARENT PAC ☐ Cassette ☐ Record	$29.95
	SPECIAL TA BOOKLETS	
	Becoming the Way We Are	$2.95
	Introduce Yourself to TA	$1.25
	Introduce Your Marriage to TA	$1.50
	TA Made Simple	$1.00

Order	CASSETTES, RECORDS, POSTERS	Retail
	Natural Breast Enlargement Cassette	$9.95
	The Parent Book 45-minute cassette	$9.95
	TA for Tots 55-minute cassette	$9.95
	TA for Kids 45-minute cassette	$9.95
	TA for Teens 45-minute cassette	$9.95
	TA for Management 45-minute cassette	$9.95
	Songs of the Warm Fuzzy LP Album ("ALL ABOUT YOUR FEELINGS")	$5.95
	RELAX FOR HEALTH CASSETTES:	
	Side A: Introduction to Hypnosis Side B: Induction, Weight Control	$9.95
	Side A: Introduction to Hypnosis Side B: Induction, Tobacco Control	$9.95
	Side A: Introduction to Hypnosis Side B: Induction, Ego Strengthening	$9.95
	Today I'm OK (4-color Poster) 6 / $5.00	$1.00
	Warm Fuzzies (min. order 50)	$.50 ea.
	Warm Fuzzy Club Membership	$4.00
	SUBTOTAL	
	MINIMUM ORDER $10.00	
	CA Residents add Sales Tax	
	Add Shipping/Handling	
	TOTAL	

*Special Offer to Schools
Classroom set (minimum 30) of TA for TOTS, TA for TOTS VOL. II, TA for KIDS or TA for TEENS available at 20% Discount.

Special Half-Price Sale
TA for Tots, Kids and Teens, plus Joy of Backpacking: books with slightly damaged covers at half-price in lots of 30 or more books. Orders of 100 or more available at 66% Discount.
Enclose this notice with your order.